8/29/09

Kip,

With Appreciation for your part in all God is doing through the ministry of Forward Edge. You are truly an example of love in action. Eph. 2:10

LOVE IN ACTION

Acknowledgments

About this book.

Love in Action™ is one of the most unique book projects ever conceived. It started with a simple idea: Cameras are a staple item for most volunteers and this results in a lot of amazing photos taken by a lot of different people—many of which would be worthy of publishing in a fine-art, coffee-table book.

Knowing that thousands of great photos would be submitted, the question was then posed: How do we pick the best from the rest? We decided to put the editing power in the hands of the people. People who understand the mission behind the photo. People just like you.

Through an immersive online experience, we asked ordinary people like photographers, doctors, union workers, musicians, moms, right-handed people...anyone from any walk of life, to vote for what they considered to be the photos that best capture the essence of volunteer service, showing love through action on the mission field. From 1,737 photo submissions, almost 50,000 votes helped shape what you hold in your hands. It's a unique concept, publishing by vote, and a unique book that will move you.

How to use this book.

Open. Enjoy the photos of ordinary people experiencing extraordinary purpose through service. Repeat. There are a few little details you might like to pay special attention to. First, be sure to check out the prize winners in the back of the book (also marked with ★ throughout). You'll also want to watch the DVD. It's got more than a thousand photos on it! Here's the caption style so you can be sure to understand what's going on in each photo:

PHOTO TITLE *(location on page):* Caption, mostly verbatim as submitted. 📷 PHOTOGRAPHER

Copyright info.

Table of Contents

In the same way, let your light shine before men, that they may see your good deeds and praise your Father in heaven.

– *Matthew 5:16*

Forward Edge International

We live in a world plagued by crises and desperate human need. Natural disasters, war, poverty, preventable diseases; these and other calamities kill thousands daily, and leave millions struggling to survive. Yet there is hope.

We were designed to make unique and significant contributions to God's purposes in the world: to bring His love, truth, mercy and compassion to the sick, the widowed, the fatherless and poor. We are "hard-wired" to show Christ's love through our actions. The Bible says we are "Christ's workmanship, created in Christ Jesus for good works which God prepared in advance for us to do" (Eph. 2:10).

Since 1983, Forward Edge International (FEI) has been mobilizing ordinary people to bring Christ's love to those affected by poverty, disaster and sickness in the U.S. and around the world. Every year, hundreds "step onto the forward edge" to support long-term relief and development projects that literally change lives, bringing hope to the hurting, comfort to the devastated, and mercy to the marginalized and overlooked.

To illustrate Forward Edge International's mission, founder and president, Joe Anfuso, often tells the story of a man with a bucket of water approaching a building engulfed in flames. Near the building is a row of sleeping firemen. The man must make a choice: Does he throw his water on the building, or on the row of sleeping firemen?

Forward Edge International has made its choice: we are waking up the firemen! By mobilizing more than a thousand short-term volunteers every year to participate firsthand in long-term Forward Edge projects, we empower individuals, churches, campus fellowships and businesses to be "the hands and feet of Jesus" in a world desperate for His touch. We believe everyone should have an opportunity to change a life. It is a unique part of Forward Edge International's mission, and something that distinguishes us from other similar organizations.

1983 TEAM *(above):* The first Forward Edge team. Photo taken in Italy. ◉ FORWARD EDGE

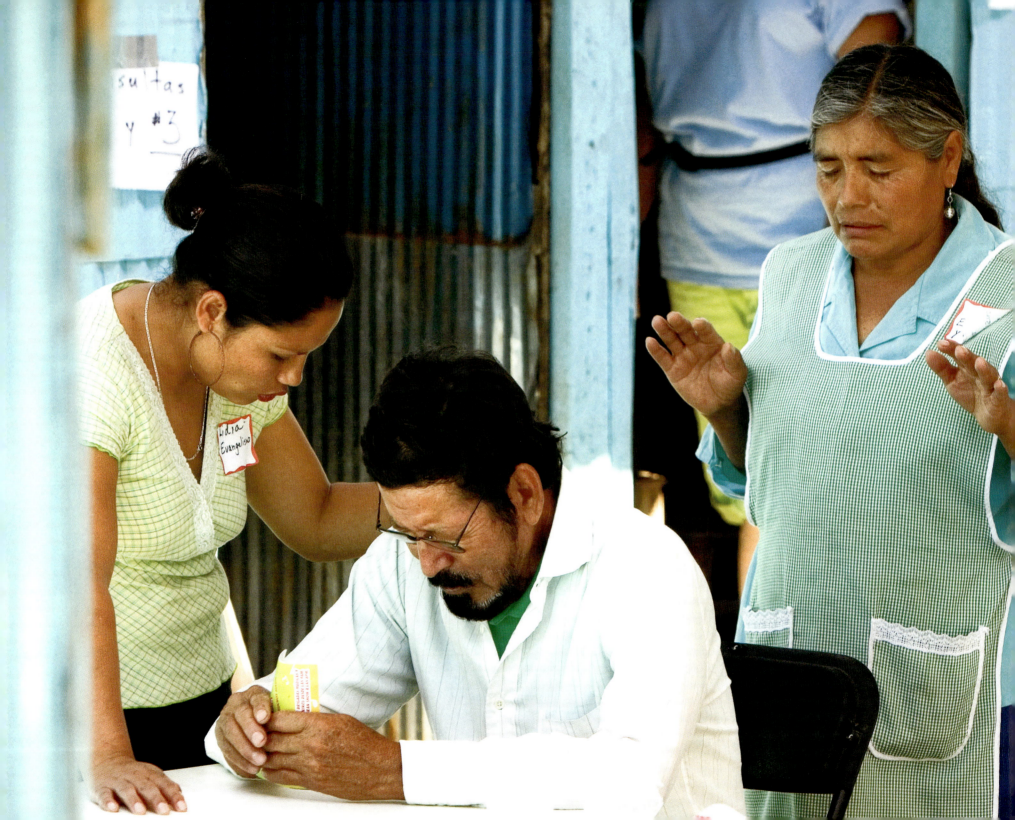

Celebrating 25 Years of Love in Action

- Hundreds of vulnerable children have been given the opportunity to reach their God-given potential through programs that meet their physical, spiritual and educational needs.

- More than 10,000 victims of natural and manmade disasters have been met in their hour of need and given food, shelter and renewed hope.

- Thousands afflicted by illness, disease or physical deformity have had their bodies healed, their sight restored, and their smiles corrected.

- More than 11,000 individuals and hundreds of churches have gained a biblical worldview through firsthand participation in front-line relief and community development projects.

Mirroring Jesus' words, tens of thousands are seeing the compassion of Christ's followers and praising our Father in heaven.

Forward Edge is not just another humanitarian organization. Foundational to this work is the belief that every person is called to reach outside themselves to serve others, to actively participate in addressing the needs of the most vulnerable among us.

NEPAL (above): FEI Founder, Joe Anfuso (left kneeling), with gospel-distribution team in the Himalayan Mountains of Nepal. Photo taken in Nepal. ◉ FORWARD EDGE

PRAYERS (opposite): Medical team offering spiritual and physical healing. Photo taken in Oaxaca, Mexico. ◉ KRIS BLAIS

FEI Milestones

1983 ....FEI is founded

1983 .... 1st FEI team, Prado, Italy

1984 ....Billy Graham Crusade, Birmingham, UK

1985 ....1st medical team, Nicaragua

1987 .... 1st teams to Asia, China and Nepal

1987 ....1st dental team, Guatemala

1987-1989 ....Children's homes constructed in Guatemala and Nicaragua

1988 ....1st team to Native American Reservation, Rosebud Sioux

1992 ....1st disaster relief team, Hurricane Andrew, Florida

1992 ....Team to Moscow after fall of Iron Curtain

1999 .... Outreach to widows and orphans after Balkan War in Kosovo

1999 ....Earthquake disaster relief, El Salvador

2000	Hurricane Mitch disaster relief in Nicaragua
2001	Outreach at Ground Zero in NYC after 9/11 attack
2004	Indian Ocean Tsunami disaster relief, Sri Lanka
2005-2009	Hurricane Katrina disaster relief
2005	1st ophthalmology team, Oaxaca, Mexico
2006-present	Program for vulnerable children, Kijabe, Kenya
2007	Construction started on *Villa Esperanza*, Managua, Nicaragua
2007	Hurricane Felix disaster relief, Puerto Cabezas, Nicaragua
2007-2009	Northwest flood disaster relief, Lewis County, Washington
2008	1st 16 girls move into *Villa Esperanza*, Managua, Nicaragua
2008	Medical team performs 100 surgeries, Puerto Cabezas, Nicaragua
2008	Luis Palau Festival, Oaxaca, Mexico

GETTING THERE

The process of arriving on the mission field can be a bit of a challenge. Going where the need is greatest often means traveling off the beaten path. Volunteer experiences include sleeping in airports, hiking remote trails, riding camels and donkeys, or paddling down rivers in dug-out canoes. The road is long, but the destination is always more than worth the journey.

CAMEL RIDE (*above*): On the way to the Dead Sea we hitched a ride by camel. Photo taken in Israel.
📷 JANICE BARNETT

RIVERBOAT (*left*): This boat takes teams up the Itaya river one hour to a remote village full of rescued street boys. Photo taken in Iquitos, Peru.
📷 CARMA ROETCISOENDER

★ **MOUNTAIN PASS** (*far left*): We traveled by train through the Swiss Alps in the Fall of 2005. It was a wonderful experience to stand at the top of Pilatus and view nothing but snow-capped mountains as far as you could see. I was humbled and reminded of the splendor in all that God has created. Photo taken in Luzerne, Switzerland.
📷 JANICE BARNETT

EL CANYON ADVENTURE
(top right): Stuck in the mud.
Photo taken in El Canyon,
Nicaragua. 📷 TJ BROOM

IS THIS SAFE? *(bottom right)*: A
pedestrian bridge in Bolivia,
South America. Photo taken in
Bolivia. 📷 FORWARD EDGE

★ **A SLIPPERY SLOPE**
(far right): With the Great Rift
Valley in the distance, volunteers
make their way down a slope
that becomes very dangerous
during the rainy season, when
the red clay becomes slick.
Photo taken in Kijabe, Kenya.
📷 CHELSEA HINDLEY

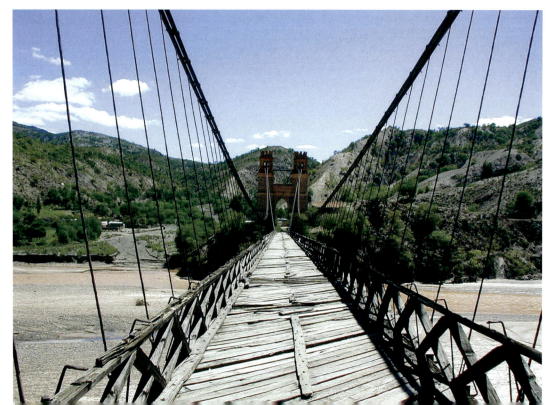

VIEW FROM THE TOP (*above*): A Forward Edge medical team in Ecuador enjoys the ride. Photo taken in Ecuador.
📷 FORWARD EDGE

LAKE-WORTHINESS (*top left*): Boats on Lake Victoria we took to an island orphanage. Photo taken in Lake Victoria, Uganda.
📷 DUSTIN RAGLAND

★ **WANT A RIDE?** (*bottom left*): Major mode of transportation... Photo taken in Mexico. 📷 MARILYN AFFOLTER

UNTITLED (*opposite*): Traffic in Kitali, Kenya.
📷 JEFF AND KRIS THOMPSON

CULTURE

Experiencing the distinctive culture of a region is one of the many blessings of travel. Because traveling for missions involves close interaction with locals, one is often able to experience the culture in a very tangible and unique way. Enjoy the sights, sounds, smells, tastes and experiences captured by many of our traveling volunteers.

HISTORIC YELLOW BUILDING *(right)*: The historic architecture in Granada is simply breathtaking! Photo taken in Granada, Nicaragua. 📷 TYLER SPEED

YAD VASHEM *(opposite)*: A surreal moment caught outside Jerusalem's holocaust museum, Yad Vashem, in May of 2008. This random man stood in quiet reflection and prayer. Photo taken in Jerusalem, Israel. 📷 JANICE BARNETT

THE SHUK *(previous left)*: A variety of spices for sale at the local marketplace in Jerusalem called the Shuk. Photo taken in Jerusalem, Israel. 📷 JANICE BARNETT

WATERMELON MAN *(previous middle)*: The colorful people at the market in Gjakova. Photo taken in Gjakova, Kosova. 📷 DONNA MOEN

MASAI GIRLS *(previous top right)*: Masai girls before showing us their cultural dance. Photo taken in Amboseli, Kenya. 📷 MARGARET PRATT

COLORFUL HAMMOCKS AT THE MARKET *(previous bottom right)*: Hammocks and more at the market. Photo taken in Managua, Nicaragua. 📷 LAURIE MCDOWELL

WALKING HOME *(above)*: They were just walking home from work. Photo taken in La Chureca, Managua, Nicaragua. 📷 KRIS BLAIS

★ **NAPPING POOCH** *(left)*: The heat, flies, smells, and sounds didn't seem to bother this dog in La Chureca. Photo taken in La Chureca, Managua, Nicaragua. 📷 MATT HARRIS

DON'T TOUCH ME *(following top left)*: This is not meant to keep people or animals in or out. This is how they get their electricity in many areas of Nicaragua. Photo taken in La Chureca, Managua, Nicaragua. 📷 CARL LACASSE

THE JOY OF COOKING *(following bottom left)*: Preparing food for a feast. Photo taken in Betkasia, Bangladesh. 📷 GAIL DALL

UNTITLED *(following middle)*: A parrot kept us company at the pastor's house in Puerto Cabezas, Nicaragua. Photo taken in Puerto Cabezas, Nicaragua. 📷 ALEXANDRA GRACE TAYLOR

MONTE ALBAN *(following right)*: These ruins date back to long before the Aztec period in Oaxaca, Mexico. Photo taken in Oaxaca, Mexico. 📷 CARL LACASSE

★ **MASAI WOMEN** (*above*): Masai women in Kenya singing for their Western visitors. Photo taken in Kenya. 📷 RYAN ANFUSO

ARISING LION (*left*): Lion waking up. Photo taken in Masai Mara, Kenya. 📷 MARGARET PRATT

THE NAKED TREE (*far left*): The beautiful naked tree. Photo taken in Masai Mara, Kenya. 📷 MARGARET PRATT

UNTITLED (*above*): The potter. Photo taken in Nicaragua. 📷 KIMBERLIE HAGGSTROM

WASHING DAY (*right*): In Vicente Guerrero, this family decided to bring out their washing and watch the activity as we poured concrete flooring for the neighbors. Photo taken in Oaxaca, Mexico. 📷 PERRI KELLY

GATHERING WOOD (*opposite*): An afternoon of gathering wood. Photo taken in Leon, Nicaragua. 📷 MARK BURTON

NATURAL MADE COLORS (*above*): The colors used to make wool carpets and clothing are made from plants, insects and lime. Photo taken in Teotitlan, Mexico. 📷 CARL LACASSE

DYES FROM THE EARTH (*left*): The colors added to the virgin wool are from plants and insects. Lime is added to activate the colors, and dipping the fabric lets the oxygen work to produce a deeper color. Photo taken in Teotitlan, Mexico. 📷 CARL LACASSE

LOBSTERS (*far left*): Lobster fisherman. Photo taken in Placencia, Belize. 📷 ELIZABETH MCCARTHY

29

MOTHERS *(above)*: Tarahumaran mothers carry their children throughout their day. Photo taken in Sierra Tarahumara Mountains, Mexico.
📷 NATHANIEL WIECK

UNTITLED *(right)*: Every door is a store. Photo taken in Rwanda.
📷 JEFF AND KRIS THOMPSON

FLOWER SELLER *(far right)*: A maker of beauty. Photo taken in Mexico. 📷 MARILYN AFFOLTER

LITTLE DANCER (*above*): A young Native American dancer at Montana's Crow Fair. Photo taken in Montana. 📷 KEVIN FONG

THE PACK OF CARDS (*left*): The locals call this street "The Pack of Cards." It overlooks the harbor of Cobh, formerly Queenstown. Hundreds of thousands of men and women left Ireland for North America from this port town, including those aboard the infamous Titanic. Photo taken in Cobh, Ireland. 📷 JANICE BARNETT

★ **DOOR OF MEXICO** (*following left*): Time had created pieces of artwork wherever one looked. Photo taken in San Miquel de Allende, Mexico. 📷 MARILYN AFFOLTER

MAIN STREET (*following right*): A bumpy road. Photo taken in Augustin Gonzales, Mexico. 📷 MARILYN AFFOLTER

CHILDREN

FEI volunteers have shown vulnerable children their love through simple actions like hugs and play-time, and by building orphanages, schools, and homes. Most recently, FEI built a Village of Hope called *Villa Esperanza* in Managua, Nicaragua, which is home to girls rescued from the nearby landfill. FEI now supports this village and the children living there, and is committed to their long-term care. In Kenya, FEI has joined forces with Mama Beth, helping to feed over 60 children daily. In addition to meals, Mama Beth supplies food for the soul by teaching these children about the love of Christ.

The blessings found through interaction with little children are priceless. The amazing vulnerability and strength in the faces that follow is breathtaking and life-changing. No matter where in the world one serves, the faces of these children melt hearts while bringing the greatest joy.

HAPPY (*top left*): She had us wait just so she could show us her puppy! Photo taken in La Chureca, Managua, Nicaragua. 📷 KRIS BLAIS

UNTITLED (*bottom left*): Gorgeous girls in a gypsy village in Romania. Photo taken in Romania. 📷 CEMELE VAUGHN

UNTITLED (*far left*): They played so hard, and then slept so well on the way home! Photo taken in Managua, Nicaragua. 📷 KRIS BLAIS

PONDERING BOY (*previous left*): The little boy was standing in front of his home in the Masai village. Photo taken in Amboseli, Kenya. 📷 MARGARET PRATT

EYES (*previous middle*): Nicaraguan child. Photo taken in Nicaragua. 📷 KIMBERLIE HAGGSTROM

LET ME IN! (*previous right*): Antoni wanted so desperately to come inside the school. Photo taken in La Chureca, Managua, Nicaragua. 📷 KRIS BLAIS

UNTITLED (*following left*): Children of Nicaragua. Photo taken in Nicaragua. 📷 KIMBERLIE HAGGSTROM

BEAUTY IN THE BREAKDOWN (*following right*): Leaving La Chureca "The Dump." Photo taken in Managua, Nicaragua. 📷 MELISSA MILLER

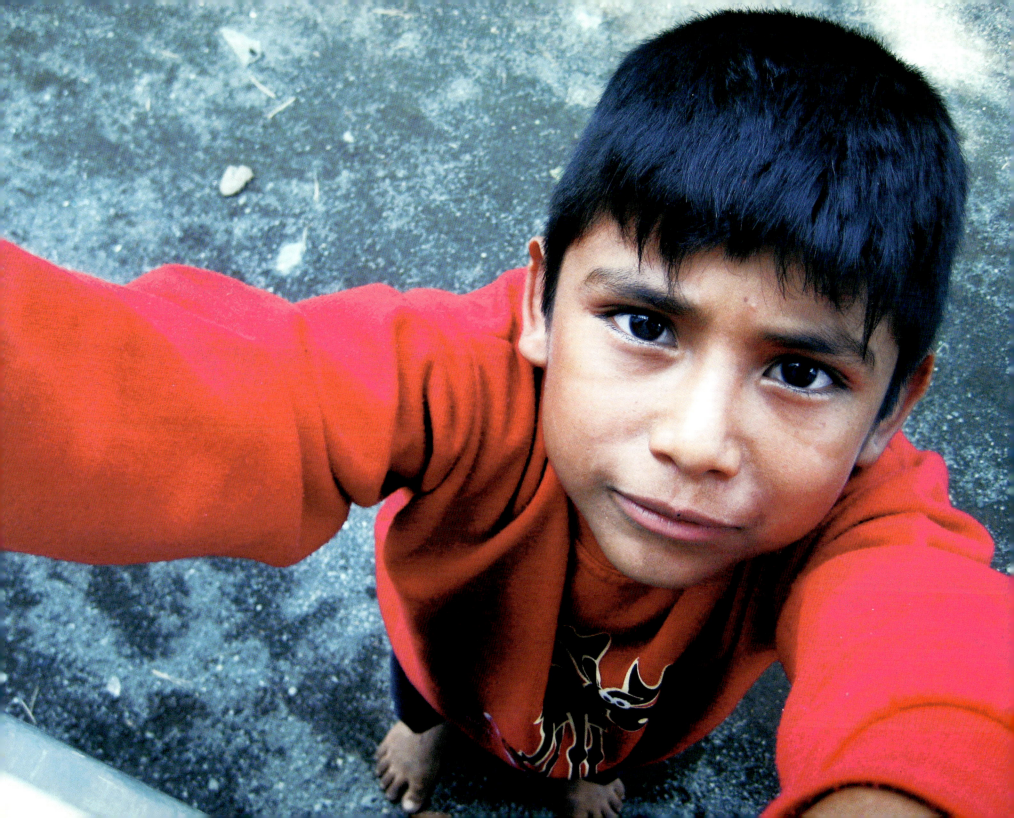

FRIENDS *(above)*: Our group has had the privilege of watching these boys grow up over the past four years. I pray that we will see them grow into men of God. Photo taken in Dominican Republic. 📷 ALYSON ROLLINS

JOY THROUGH A SMILE *(right)*: Though Johnny's physical disabilities may restrain him from many activities, it will never take away the wonderful smile he displays. Photo taken in Puerto Plata, Dominican Republic. 📷 ALYSON ROLLINS

FREE *(previous left)*: We took several kids from La Chureca to the beach. For many of them it was their first time. We rode horses and ATV's, played in the water and ate ice cream. Photo taken in Managua, Nicaragua. 📷 KRIS BLAIS

UNTITLED *(previous right)*: Boy from the dump in Nicaragua. Photo taken in La Chureca, Managua, Nicaragua. 📷 KIMBERLIE HAGGSTROM

KIDS WANT TO HAVE FUN *(following top left)*: To know some of these children and to know the miracles in their lives is precious. Saul, second from the right, has severe scoliosis. What a beautiful child. Photo taken in Oaxaca, Mexico. 📷 CARL LACASSE

UNTITLED *(following middle left)*: Leyli loves to swing! Photo taken in Vida Nueva, Managua, Nicaragua. 📷 KRIS BLAIS

FINGERNAIL TIME! *(following bottom left)*: This picture shows that the children at the orphanage have come to see each other as brothers and sisters even though there is no blood relation. Photo taken in El Cañón Orphanage, Nicaragua. 📷 ALYSON ROLLINS

UNTITLED *(following middle)*: Our team spent a few days in Betania, which was suffering from the hurricane that hit in 2007. We worked to build houses for the families and played soccer with the children. These boys enjoyed giving and getting piggy-back rides, and sharing smiles all around. Photo taken in Betania, Nicaragua. 📷 ALEXANDRA GRACE TAYLOR

★ **UNTITLED** *(following right)*: A child's smile lifts my soul no matter where I am. Photo taken in Rwanda. 📷 JEFF AND KRIS THOMPSON

EL NINO AZUL (*right*): A boy whose home we were building. Photo taken in Nuevo Progreso, Mexico.
📷 DUSTIN RAGLAND

★ **FRANKLIN** (*far right*): When my team spent time at the orphanage in Puerto Cabezas, I got to know Franklin as I struggled to speak in Spanish. He was full of joy and hugs, and always put a smile on my face. I hope I can visit him again. Photo taken in Puerto Cabezas, Nicaragua.
📷 ALEXANDRA GRACE TAYLOR

UNTITLED (*below*): Curious. Photo taken in Don Bosco, Domincan Republic.
📷 DONNA MOEN

WENDI AND ANTONI *(above):* They were always up for a Kodak moment! Photo taken in La Chureca, Managua, Nicaragua. 📷 KRIS BLAIS

HAIR! *(left):* This precious barrio girl had so much hair and even more personality. Photo taken in Dominican Republic. 📷 MELEAH SMITH

★ **BATH TIME** *(far left):* No matter what country, bath time always turns into play time with bubbles. Photo taken in El Cañón Orphanage, Nicaragua. 📷 ALYSON ROLLINS

TIME TO SLEEP (*above*): This beautiful little abandoned baby lives in the hospital I volunteer at. She has spent all 2 years of her life living in the hospital. Photo taken in Oradea-Mare, Bihor. 📷 RACHEL TITIRIGA

BEAUTIFUL PRAYERS! (*right*): How beautiful are the prayers of children. "But God has surely listened and heard my voice in prayer. Praise be to God, who has not rejected my prayer or withheld his love from me!" (Psalm 66:19-20)This beautiful girl lives in a small community known as Cangrejo. Photo taken in Puerto Plata, Dominican Republic. 📷 ALYSON ROLLINS

FRIENDSHIP (*far right*): These were kids from the gypsy village in Sabolch. 📷 BECCA MASHBURN

SHY FOR THE CAMERA (*opposite*): She giggled! She hid her head...and she kept on giggling. Photo taken in Augustin Gonzales, Mexico. 📷 MARILYN AFFOLTER

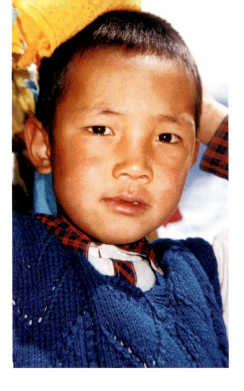

TIBETAN BOY (*above*): A young Tibetan boy near Jokhang Temple in the heart of Lhasa. Photo taken in Lhasa, Tibet. 📷 HEATHER BAKER

CURIOUS (*top right*): Kids want their picture taken so they can see themselves on the camera screen. Photo taken in Kijabe, Kenya. 📷 AMY UDELL

FRIENDS (*bottom right*): These close friends pose for their picture! Photo taken in Kijabe, Kenya. 📷 AMY UDELL

SCHOOL WORK (*far right*): A day at school. Photo taken in Leon, Nicaragua. 📷 CRYSTAL CARBONE

HELPING OUT (*previous left*): This boy was glad to help volunteers building his neighbor a new home, even though he himself needed a new home. Photo taken in Kijabe, Kenya. 📷 AMY UDELL

JUST WATCHING (*previous right*): These children gather to watch volunteers build a fellow villager a new home. Photo taken in Kijabe, Kenya. 📷 AMY UDELL

PROUD (*left*): She was so excited to invite me into her house. Photo taken in La Chureca, Managua, Nicaragua. KRIS BLAIS

UNTITLED (*far left*): He slept through his first time at the beach! Photo taken in Managua, Nicaragua. KRIS BLAIS

LITTLE GIRLS PLAYING IN THE CITY DUMP (*following top left*): There was a big difference in the appearance of the children we saw at the clinic, compared to those walking around La Chureca. They were happy to come over and say hello. Photo taken in La Chureca, Managua, Nicaragua. LAURIE MCDOWELL

BUBBLE GIRL (*following bottom left*): She was so surprised when the bubbles floated in front of her. Photo taken in Vida Nueva, Managua, Nicaragua. KRIS BLAIS

CATALINA AND HER BEAUTY (*following top right*): Catalina of Leon is a true miracle. When she was very small she fell from a horse and was then kicked in the head. Photo taken in Leon, Nicaragua. CARL LACASSE

ONE OF GOD'S ANGELS (*following bottom right*): A peaceful moment while mother was waiting to seek some medical attention in Oaxaca. Photo taken in Oaxaca, Mexico. CARL LACASSE

KIDS SHOOTING MARBLES (*following right*): Kids shooting marbles in La Cumbre, Oaxaca, Mexico at 9,000 feet above sea level. Photo taken in La Cumbre, Oaxaca, Mexico in September 2008. RONNY GILMORE

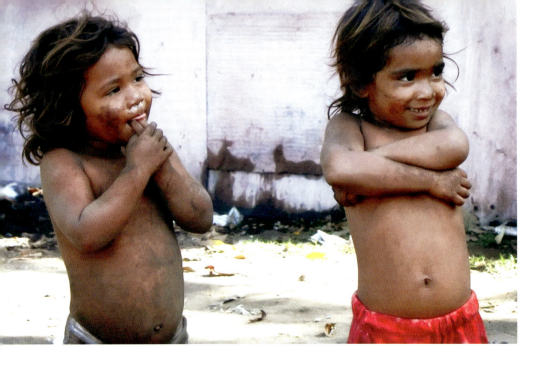

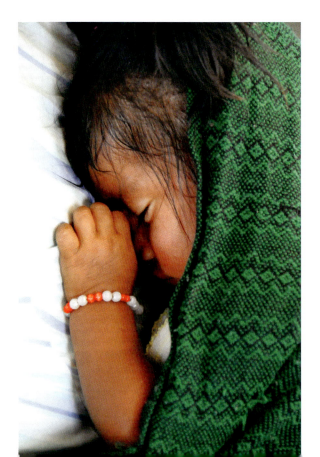

UNTITLED *(above):* Lunch is so much fun, when you have something to eat. Photo taken in Rwanda. 📷 JEFF AND KRIS THOMPSON

HOLA *(left):* She doesn't fear the barbed wire she is holding on to. Photo taken in Leon, Nicaragua. 📷 CARL LACASSE

LAUGHTER *(following left):* Volunteer, Janette Mahew, of Rolling Hills Community Church in Tualatin, OR, plays with a vibrant group of children in the projects near Moss Point, MS. Photo taken in Moss Point, MS. 📷 KATHLEEN NYBERG

HOPE *(following right):* Portrait of a young girl, displaced by Katrina, in Moss Point, MS. Photo taken in Moss Point, MS. 📷 KATHLEEN NYBERG

DISASTER RELIEF

Victims of natural and manmade disasters—hurricanes, earthquakes, tsunamis, war—experience a sudden and devastating upheaval of their lives. In the immediate days following an event, they are often without adequate food, water, shelter or medical care. But the devastating effects of a disaster do not go away in a matter of weeks or months. It is often years before victims return to any form of normalcy, if they ever return. We see this as a unique opportunity for God's people to be His hand extended at a time when many are losing hope and desperate for God's mercy.

FEI volunteers respond with support, love, and help. The devastation is only the beginning of a story that ends with people loving, supporting and offering hope to those hurting. You will find here devastation and celebration as people experience hope and love through the actions of short-term volunteers.

AFTER *(above)*: A destroyed kitchen in New Orleans after Hurricane Katrina. Photo taken in New Orleans, LA. 📷 KRIS BLAIS

DISCOVERED TREASURE *(top right)*: FEI Facilitator, Suzie Smith, reads a Bible uncovered in a Sri Lankan home destroyed by the Indian Ocean Tsunami. Photo taken in Sri Lanka. 📷 DOUG CRANE

TSUNAMI WRECKAGE *(bottom right)*: Sri Lankan fishing boats swept ashore by the Indian Ocean Tsunami in 2004. Photo taken in Sri Lanka. 📷 DOUG CRANE

THE SHACK *(far right)*: Some of the village boys of Betania were watching as their new house was being built. Photo taken in Betania, Nicaragua. 📷 CARL LACASSE

THE CALVARY IS HERE *(previous left)*: Here comes our supplies and labor to help rebuild Betania. The village of Betania was destroyed by Hurricane Felix in 2007. Photo taken in Betania, Nicaragua. 📷 CARL LACASSE

SORROW *(previous top)*: Sometimes life is simply more than we can bear. Photo taken in Kauai, Hawaii. 📷 JANICE BARNETT

RECLINER *(previous bottom)*: One year after Hurricane Katrina, many buildings near the Lower 9th Ward still looked as though the storm hit yesterday. Photo taken in New Orleans, LA. 📷 KATHLEEN NYBERG

GROUND ZERO AT NIGHT *(above)*: Ground Zero at night just after sunset. Photo taken in New York City. 📷 Carl LaCasse

★ **POWER** *(top)*: This church in Gulfport, Mississippi shows the power of Hurricane Katrina really well. It amazes me that wind and rain can take out such a strong wall. Photo taken in Gulfport, Mississippi, USA. 📷 ASHLEY SHORT

★ **DARVIN & MADONNA** *(left)*: Darvin and Madonna stand in the remains of their swimming pool in Mississippi, one year after surviving Hurricane Katrina. Photo taken in Mississippi. 📷 KATHLEEN NYBERG

★ **A PHOTO ALBUM** *(far left)*: Could you imagine if this is what happened to your most treasured possessions? Photo taken in Lower 9th Ward, New Orleans, LA. 📷 KRIS BLAIS

VOLUNTEERS

Short-term missions and volunteer work is truly a great vehicle for God to use ordinary people to reach out to those in need. FEI mobilizes hundreds of individuals each year to show Christ's love through their actions; helping volunteers experience extraordinary purpose.

So many ordinary people have willingly left their comfort zones to serve others. As you page through this chapter enjoy this glimpse into the life-changing experience of reaching out to vulnerable children, populations in desperate need of health care, and those affected by disaster.

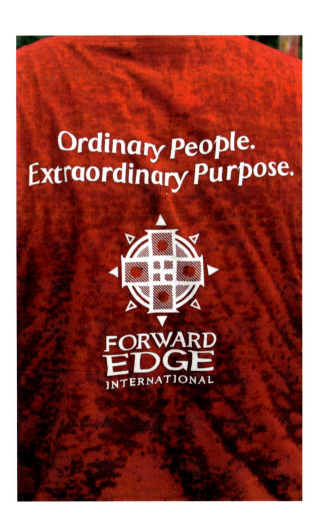

DIRT CAN'T HURT *(above)*: Dirt is something that can be washed away, but the relationships built will last forever! Photo taken in Leon, Nicaragua. 📷 ALYSON ROLLINS

GIVING *(left)*: The one sitting down is Sara. She is too sick to take care of herself, so a few of the team members went and bought her a month's supply of food. Photo taken in Leon, Nicaragua. 📷 CARL LACASSE

★ **LOVE** *(previous left)*: Susie and Marcos! Photo taken in Vida Nueva, Managua, Nicaragua. 📷 KRIS BLAIS

THE SHIRT *(previous middle)*: The Forward Edge shirt after volunteering. Photo taken in Nicaragua. 📷 CRYSTAL CARBONE

THE FIGHT *(previous right)*: The real question is, who is going to win the battle for the wheelbarrow? Photo taken in El Canyon Orphanage, Nicaragua. 📷 ALYSON ROLLINS

SMILES FOR MILES *(following left)*: In the dump school, nothing could keep these three from smiling. Photo taken in La Chureca, Managua, Nicaragua. 📷 MATT HARRIS

SUPPORT *(following right)*: Dalton and Zac loved to lay in the hammock at the Villa. They were happy to share with some of the children from El Canyon. I think all four felt supported. Photo taken in *Villa Esperanza*, Managua, Nicaragua. 📷 MATT HARRIS

UNTITLED (*top left*): Kate Anfuso. Photo taken in Belize.
📷 DON MOEN

★ **PREPARATION** (*bottom left*): I was volunteering at a local children's hospital in Bucharest, Romania. I was helping to clean this room in preparation for the abandoned and orphaned children who were going to be moved here. Photo taken in Bucharest, Romania. 📷 RACHEL TITIRIGA

★ **UNTITLED** (*opposite*): New friends. Photo taken in Kijabe, Kenya. 📷 AMY UDELL

HAPPY CHILDREN (*following left*): Washing feet and giving new shoes. Photo taken in Leon, Nicaragua. 📷 CINDY AUBRY

TIEMPO PARA FUTBOL! (*following top*): Who do you think won this soccer game, Haitians or Gringos? Just look for the medals! Photo taken in Puerto Plata, Dominican Republic.
📷 ALYSON ROLLINS

DINNER TIME (*following bottom left*): Chris is feeding one of the babies at the Bagwell's orphanage. Photo taken in Managua, Nicaragua. 📷 CARL LACASSE

NURTURING A BABE (*following bottom right*): Kat is nurturing a little girl at El Canyon Orphanage. Photo taken in Managua Nicaragua. 📷 CARL LACASSE

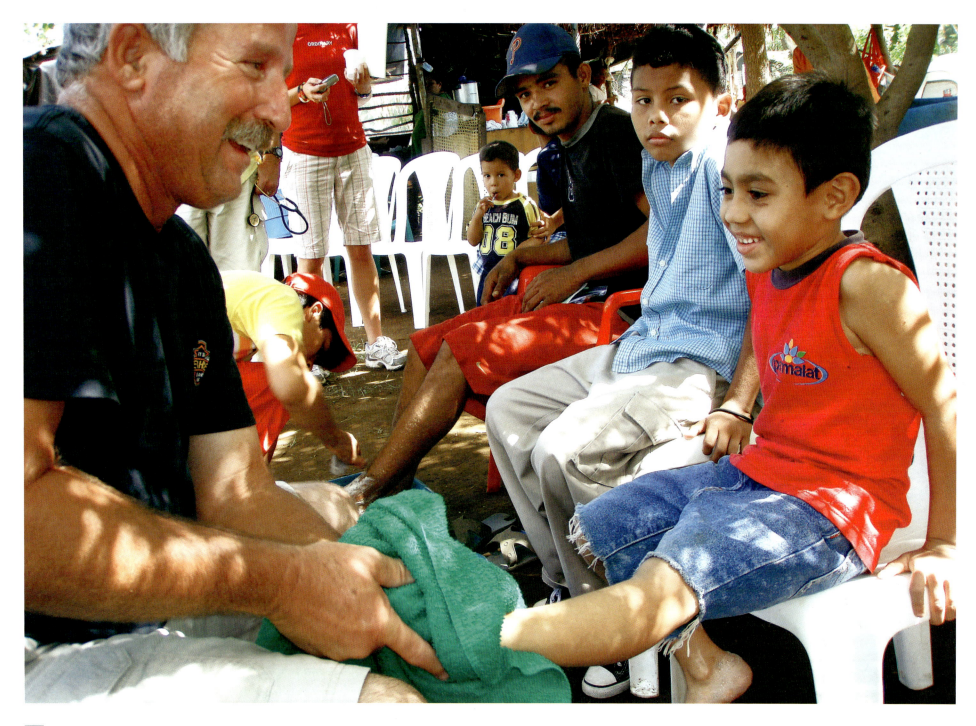

MUD BOWL *(above)*: Our first couple of days we did not have electricity or running water so the team decided to play soccer with the orphans that live on the property at the Verbo Church. Here is the aftermath, minus the cuts and scrapes. Photo taken in Puerto Cabezas, Nicaragua. 📷 CARL LACASSE

GEORGE *(left)*: George after a hard day of work at *Villa Esperanza*. Photo taken at *Villa Esperanza*, Managua, Nicaragua. 📷 CARL LACASSE

UNTITLED (top right): Jenn loved the kids at the orphanage. Then again who didn't? Photo taken in Vida Nueva, Managua, Nicaragua. 📷 KRIS BLAIS

PREACHING IN BOTH LANGUAGES (bottom right): Sean is preaching while Gloria interprets at Pastor Delores's church. Photo taken in Leon, Nicaragua. 📷 CARL LACASSE

OH JOHN BOY (far right): John Little did not know he had the touch until he held this baby at the Bagwell's baby orphanage. Photo taken in Managua, Nicaragua. 📷 CARL LACASSE

OAXACAN GOTHIC (previous left): Vicki and Jim Williams take a moment from pouring concrete floors in Oaxaca, Mexico, to pose a la "American Gothic" on their anniversary. Photo taken in Oaxaca, Mexico. 📷 PERRI KELLY

AFTER (previous middle): Volunteers with "Common Ground Relief" use machetes to hack away at grass growing persistently in yards of the Lower 9th Ward homes. Photo taken in 9th Ward, New Orleans, Louisiana. 📷 KATHLEEN NYBERG

READY SET (previous right): FEI volunteers in the Gulf Coast are ready for action. Photo taken in Gulf Coast. 📷 FORWARD EDGE

UNTITLED (following left): Volunteers and kids from La Chureca playing in the ocean together. Photo taken in Managua, Nicaragua. 📷 KRIS BLAIS

UNTITLED (following right): Day at the beach with the girls from *Villa Esperanza*. Photo taken in Managua, Nicaragua. 📷 DONNA MOEN

A MASTERPIECE? *(above):* And I wonder what the Haitians were thinking in the background. Photo taken in Puerto Plata, Dominican Republic.
📷 ALYSON ROLLINS

LOVE THROUGH A HUG *(left):* Sometimes all a child needs is love through a warm hug. Photo taken in Puerto Plata, Dominican Republic. 📷 ALYSON ROLLINS

WORSHIPING *(opposite):* The whole team worshiping during a concert at the June 2005 Billy Graham Crusade at Flushing Meadows. Photo taken in Flushing Meadows, New York. 📷 CARL LACASSE

UNTITLED *(below):* Trading instruments with a blind Tibetan. Photo taken in Tibet.
📷 DON TOFTE

WE ARE THE FEET (*above*): We are the feet! The volunteers weren't afraid to get a little dirty. Photo taken in *Villa Esperanza*, Managua, Nicaragua. 📷 KRIS BLAIS

UNTITLED (*right*): A mud and stick house in Rwanda. Photo taken in Rwanda. 📷 JEFF AND KRIS THOMPSON

HURRICANE KATRINA RELIEF (*following left*): Team Oregon putting roofs back on the community homes after Hurricane Katrina. Photo taken in Mississippi. 📷 JON WATSON

DR. DAVID ON ZIP LINE (*following right*): No fear. Photo taken in Mombacho, Volcano Canopy Tour. 📷 LAURIE MCDOWELL

UNTITLED (*right*): Just couldn't stop loving them. Photo taken in Vida Nueva, Managua, Nicaragua. 📷 KRIS BLAIS

TENDER JOY (*far right*): This sweet girl was a part of our team and is hugging a little boy who radiates with joy. Every time we see him he literally can't stop smiling. Photo taken in Dominican Republic.
📷 MELEAH SMITH

JADE (*following left*): A volunteer shows the children a photo taken of them, much to their delight. Photo taken in Betania, Nicaragua. 📷 ALEXANDRA GRACE TAYLOR

UNTITLED (*following right*): Playing at the beach! Photo taken in Managua, Nicaragua.
📷 KRIS BLAIS

CONSTRUCTION

Construction work is a literal expression of being the hands and feet of Jesus. Many volunteers, regardless of age or strength, are able to participate in helping those who require the basics, like adequate shelter. Whether repairing dump homes, providing schools for vulnerable children, or helping rebuild homes ruined by disaster, construction is a beautiful expression of Jesus caring for all the needs of His people.

PISOS *(above)*: A volunteer pours cement floors (called pisos) the old fashioned way. Photo taken in Oaxaca, Mexico. 📷 KRIS BLAIS

UNTITLED *(right)*: Preparing for a new cement floor. Photo taken in Oaxaca, Mexico. 📷 CARL LACASSE

WORKING HARD *(previous left)*: Everyone was working so hard to move that mound of dirt so the landscaping at *Villa Esperanza* would be perfect. Photo taken in Managua, Nicaragua. 📷 KRIS BLAIS

UNTITLED *(previous middle)*: RJ working hard to perfect the flooring. Photo taken in Oaxaca, Mexico. 📷 KRIS BLAIS

BUILDING *(previous right)*: Volunteers and villagers help build a home for a family in a village called Kijabe in Kenya. Photo taken in Kijabe, Kenya. 📷 AMY UDELL

ON TO THE NEXT STOP *(above)*: Every morning till late afternoon, they walked from tin shack to tin shack with a concrete mixer to pour flooring for the needy of Vicente Guerrero, a village built on the Oaxacan dump. Concrete is necessary to help stop the infestation of intestinal worms that plague the children of the village. Photo taken in Oaxaca, Mexico. 📷 PERRI KELLY

★ **THE HELPER** *(right)*: Jason Rowland, a volunteer from Fairbanks, Alaska, gets a little help hauling concrete from the young man of the house. Photo taken in Oaxaca, Mexico. 📷 PERRI KELLY

ROOF RACE *(opposite top)*: This is from the trip I went on to Hattiesburg, Mississippi in 2006. Our team was working on three houses, we removed the blue plastic on the roofs and replaced it with new tar paper and shingles. The first two were side by side so we split up into two groups and raced. 📷 ASHLEY SHORT

HARD AT WORK *(opposite bottom left)*: Painting the school. Photo taken in Flowers Bank, Belize. 📷 MARGARET PRATT

SEEING FEET AND HEARING HAMMERS *(opposite bottom right)*: Scaffolding made from two by fours and flimsy boards was a new experience for all of us but we were all excited to feel the middle give beneath us. Think of it as a trampoline! 📷 ELISHA FIELDSTADT

UNTITLED *(above)*: Just the beginning. Photo taken in Rio Blanco, Nicaragua. 📷 KATIE MCGREW

DIGGING DITCH *(left)*: Digging a ditch for electrical conduit at *Villa Esparanza*. It was 4 feet deep and 50-60 meters in length. Photo taken in Managua, Nicaragua. 📷 BOB MAURIO

★ **PAINTING** *(far left)*: Painting the curbs at the Villa. Photo taken in *Villa Esperanza*, Managua, Nicaragua. 📷 DONNA MOEN

HARD WORK (*above*): Volunteers paint a house in Nairobi Kenya. Photo taken in Nairobi, Kenya.
📷 AMY UDELL

★ **FOCUSED** (*right*): George is the "human backhoe," removing dirt from a couple buildings for some new Villa homes. Photo taken at *Villa Esperanza* in Managua, Nicaragua.
📷 CARL LACASSE

TEAM WORK (*far right*): Without God and the team, this could not be accomplished. Photo taken in Betania, Nicaragua. 📷 CARL LACASSE

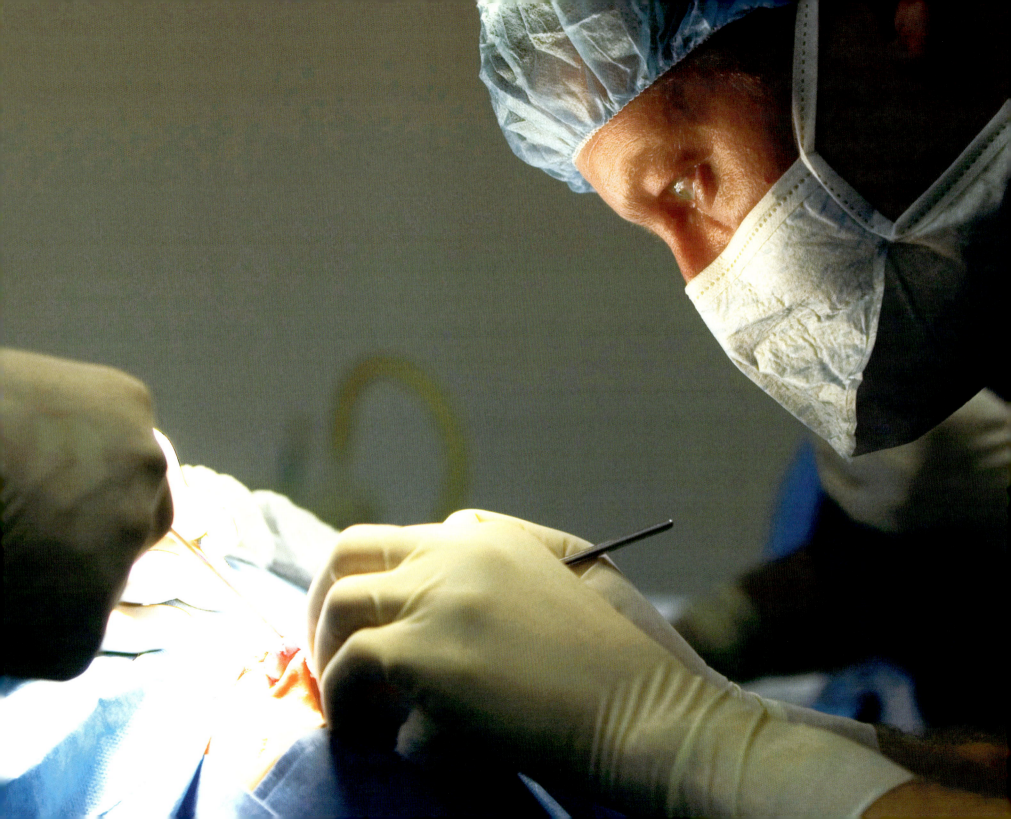

HEALTH CARE

In many developing countries, necessary health care is simply unavailable. Volunteers meet a great need by providing health care to remote and poverty-stricken areas. Dental teams, surgical teams, ophthalmologists, general practitioners and nurses have traveled the world with FEI. They provide urgently-needed care and preventative services like education and clean-water projects to the poorest of the poor. The photos here not only express the need but also how that need is being met through the actions of so many.

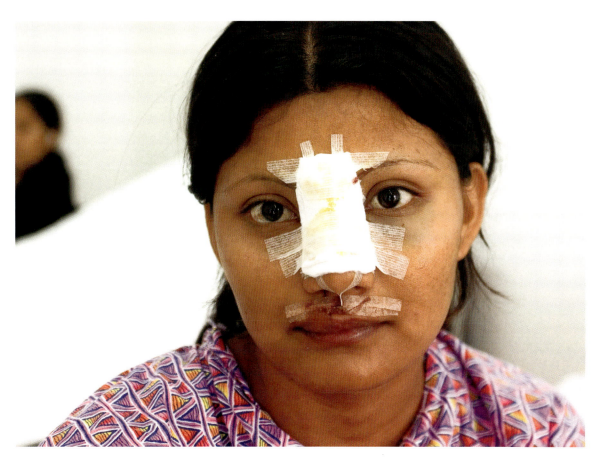

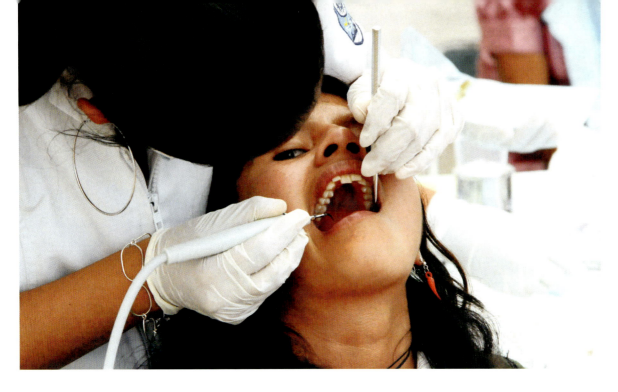

TEETH (*above*): A volunteer dentist at the 2008 Luis Palau Festival. Photo taken in Oaxaca, Mexico. 📷 CARL LACASSE

A LIFE-CHANGING GIFT (*right*): A disabled boy on Nicaragua's Atlantic Coast sits and laughs for the first time in his new donated wheelchair. Photo taken in Nicaragua. 📷 PEGGY O'NEIL

UNDER THE KNIFE (*far right*): Volunteer physicians perform a cleft palate surgery. Photo taken in Nicaragua. 📷 FORWARD EDGE

X-RAYS (*opposite*): This doctor manages with natural light in the makeshift, outdoor clinic. Photo taken in Oaxaca, Mexico. 📷 KRIS BLAIS

★ **SURGERY** (*previous left*): The intensity of the surgeon's concentration is amazing. Photo taken in Oaxaca, Mexico. 📷 KRIS BLAIS

HELPING ONE AT A TIME (*previous top left*): Supplies we brought in to help the people in Leon. Photo taken in Leon, Nicaragua. 📷 CINDY AUBRY

POST-OP (*previous bottom middle*): Photo taken in Oaxaca, Mexico. 📷 KRIS BLAIS

UNTITLED (*previous bottom right*): This was the operating room in the children's hospital we visited. You can still see some drops of blood that were left on the floor. Photo taken in Nicaragua. 📷 KIMBERLIE HAGGSTROM

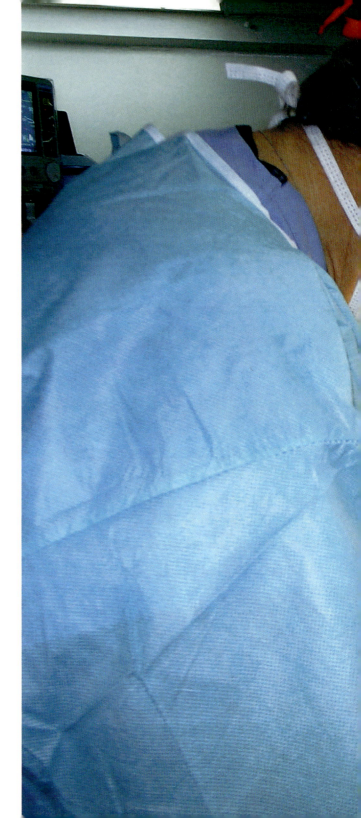

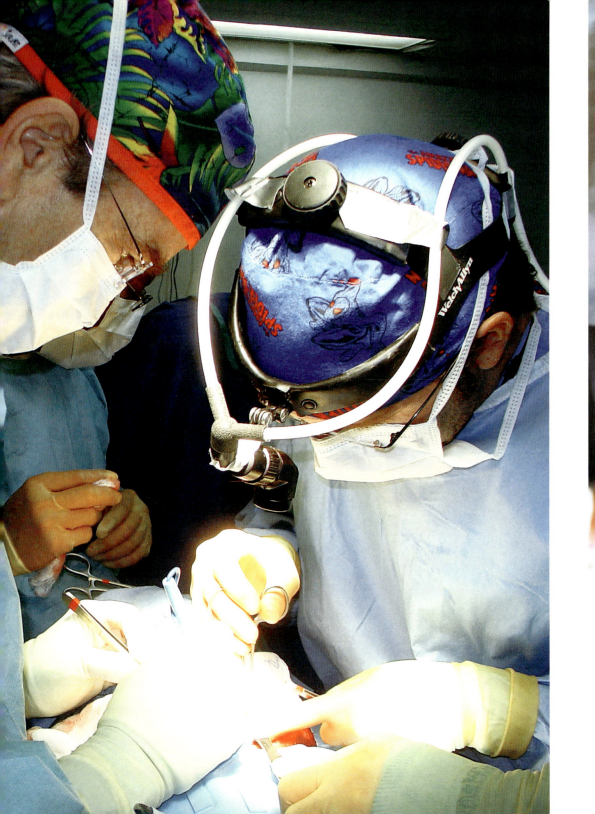
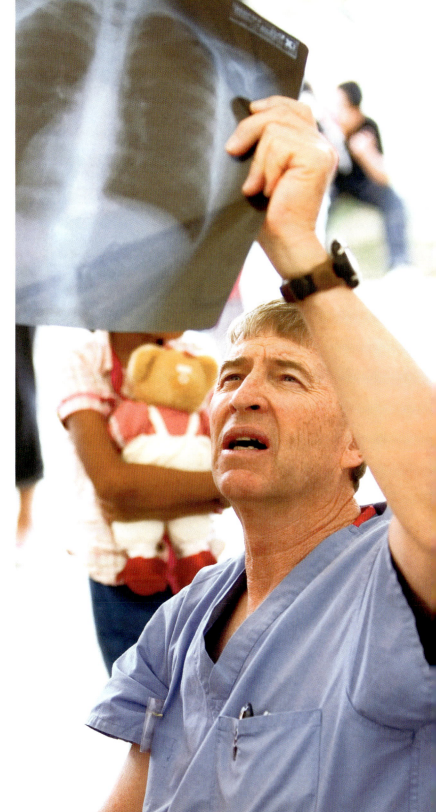

OPEN UP AND SAY "AH!" *(above):* Dr. Bergstrom examining a young patient. Photo taken in Oaxaca, Mexico. 📷 KRIS BLAIS

NEW SIGHT *(right):* A group of patients celebrate with their surgeon, Dr. Rutgard, after their successful cataract removal surgeries. Photo taken in Oaxaca, Mexico. 📷 TOM HOGAN

★ **LET ME TRY** *(far right):* Lester enjoyed imitating the doctor! Photo taken in Leon, Nicaragua. 📷 CRYSTAL CARBONE

UNTITLED *(following left):* A young child is examined by a team of volunteer doctors and nurses. Photo taken in Oaxaca, Mexico. 📷 KRIS BLAIS

★ **THE CRIPPLED MADE WELL** *(following right):* "The people were amazed when they saw the mute speaking, the crippled made well, the lame walking and the blind seeing. And they praised the God of Israel." Matthew 15:31. One day he will be running into the arms of Jesus. Jose lives at a small orphanage for children with disabilities. Photo taken in Dominican Republic. 📷 ALYSON ROLLINS

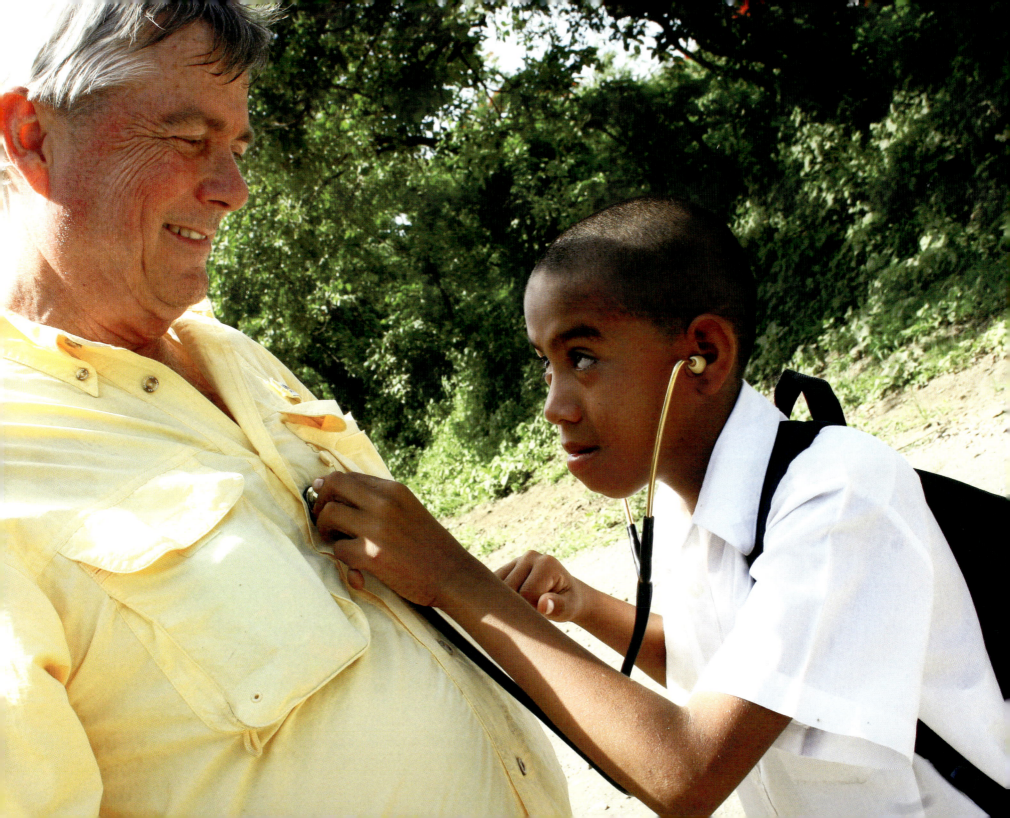

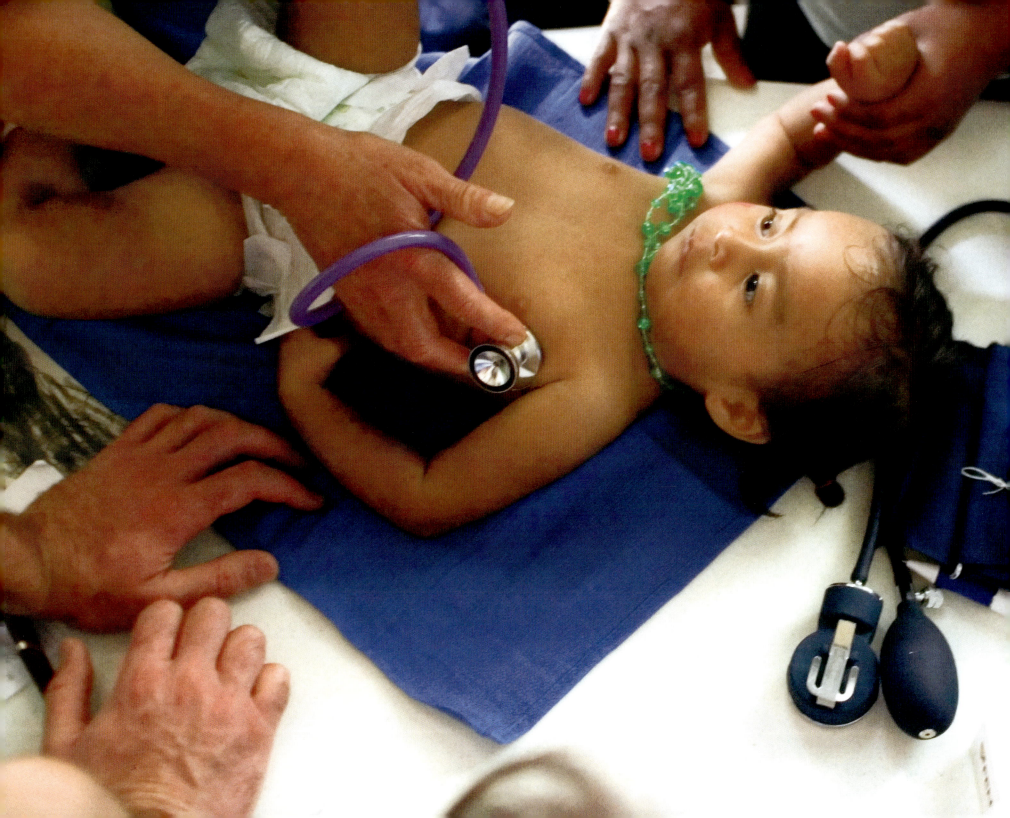

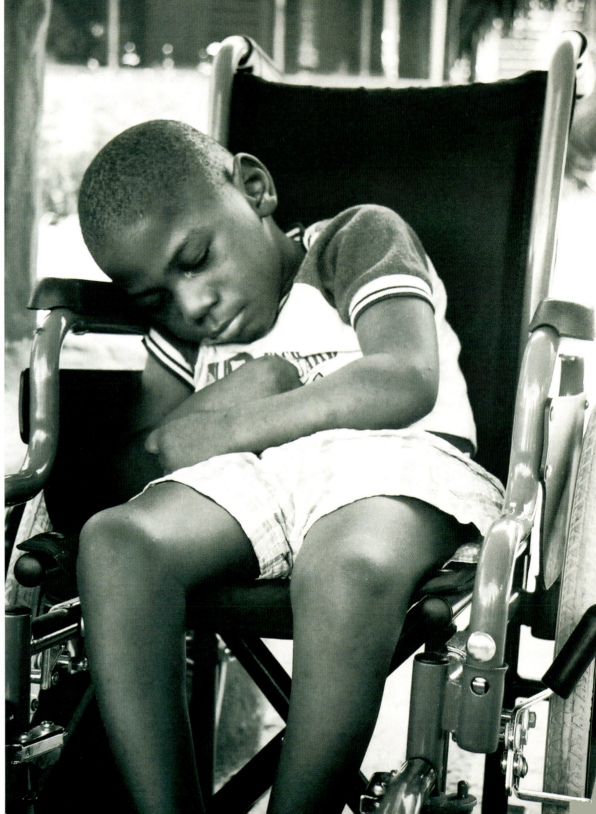

PEOPLE

When traveling the globe one is often struck by the extraordinary beauty and diversity of God's creatures. There is need, hurt, poverty and sadness etched in the lines on the faces. But there is also resilience, laughter, joy, and hope.

Each of us is uniquely and wonderfully made. The following pages display just a glimpse of our Creator's love and handiwork.

UNTITLED (*above*): The joy of the LORD is my strength!
📷 JEFF AND KRIS THOMPSON

SMILES ALOT (*top left*): Peeking through a gate, deep in one of the communities in La Chureca, this lady gave us a warm smile. Photo taken in La Chureca, Managua, Nicaragua.
📷 CARL LACASSE

SAVED (*bottom left*): In Nuevo Manantiales, Pastor Marcellino prays over a new convert while volunteer Jim Williams records the moment. This man had been hearing about children's church from his kids all week, and decided to see for himself what it was all about. He decided to give his life to Christ. Photo taken in Oaxaca, Mexico. 📷 PERRI KELLY

UNTITLED (*opposite*): This is our life. Photo taken in India.
📷 JEFF AND KRIS THOMPSON

ALEX (*previous left*): Alex was a local. He helped our team all week in Managua. Photo taken in Managua, Nicaragua.
📷 KRIS BLAIS

WISE EYES (*previous middle*): Wisdom etched in the face of an elderly woman. Photo taken in Oaxaca, Mexico.
📷 FORWARD EDGE

FINALLY HOME (*previous right*): Miss Urmatine was so happy to finally be home, after almost 3 years of being displaced. Photo taken in Lower 9th Ward, New Orleans, LA. 📷 KRIS BLAIS

BOUNTY OF COLOR (*above*): Dividing the bountiful gift of over 500 lbs. of wool, brought over in suitcases. I wonder how many customs officials raised their eyebrows over these. Photo taken in Augustin Gonzales, Mexico. 📷 MARILYN AFFOLTER

A PICTURE OF HEALTH (*right*): In Vicente Guerrero, where many children become sick with intestinal worms, this proud grandmother shows off her obviously healthy grandbaby. Photo taken in Oaxaca, Mexico. 📷 PERRI KELLY

WALK ON BY? (*far right*): It takes so little to help. Photo taken in Mexico. 📷 MARILYN AFFOLTER

★ **ONE GOD, MANY TRIBES**
(left): During the Luis Palau festival. Richard was letting the indigenous people know that it is okay to dance to our Lord. Photo taken in Oaxaca, Mexico. 📷 CARL LACASSE

OAXACAN COUPLE *(far left):* An elderly couple in a village outside Oaxaca City. Photo taken in Oaxaca, Mexico. 📷 FORWARD EDGE

ISRAELI SOLDIER *(following left):* This soldier stood watch on Mt. Kabir, the Mount of Blessings. Photo taken in Israel. 📷 JANICE BARNETT

UNTITLED *(following middle):* I have survived genocide. Photo taken in Rwanda. 📷 JEFF AND KRIS THOMPSON

GOD'S ARMY *(following right):* Waiting to go on duty, these soldiers posed for a picture. Photo taken in Jerusalem, Israel. 📷 JANICE BARNETT

125

UNTITLED (*above*): We gave this Lama new glasses and some reading material. Photo taken in Tibet. 📷 DON TOFTE

GRACE (*right*): The beauty in aging. Photo taken in Nicaragua. 📷 KIMBERLIE HAGGSTROM

HOPE (*far right*): A man at the dump who became a believer our first visit there. When we met him he was ready to kill himself. He has since become a leader in the community and church, and married the mother of his children. Photo taken in Dominican Republic. 📷 MELEAH SMITH

UNTITLED (*following left*): Photo taken in Nicaragua. 📷 KIMBERLIE HAGGSTROM

RUG HOOKING KNOWS NO BORDERS (*following right*): It's called "Rug Hooking Knows No Borders." It's another grassroots movement started, like so many others, by a group of people who care. The rugs are designed and created by the women of Augustin Gonzales, Mexico, reflections of the life around them. Proceeds from all sales go to the individual artist. Photo taken in Mexico. 📷 MARILYN AFFOLTER

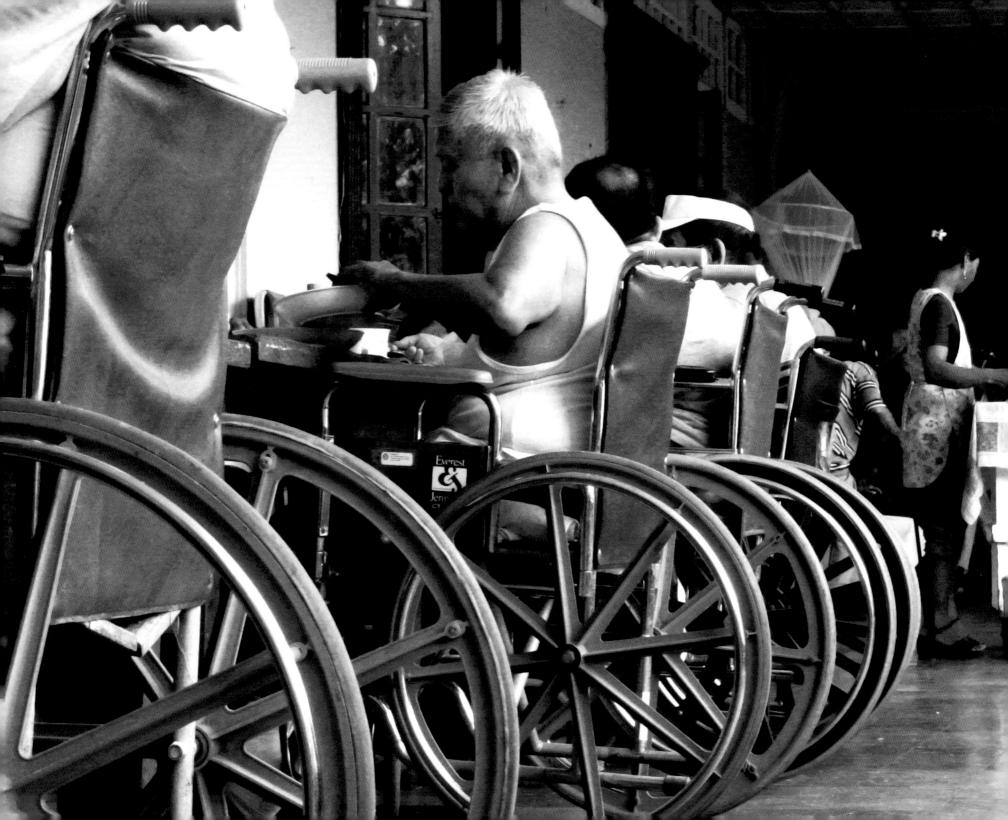

UNTITLED *(above):* Yi minority woman reading gospel pamphlet. Photo taken in China.
📷 DON TOFTE

PASSION *(left):* Pastor Charles is passionate about getting the Lower 9th Ward cleaned up. Photo taken in Lower 9th Ward, New Orleans, LA. 📷 KRIS BLAIS

ALMOST DONE! *(far left):* Linda Carter's mother's house was severely damaged by the storm. Her house is near completion thanks to the help of FEI teams! Photo taken in Lower 9th Ward, New Orleans, LA. 📷 KRIS BLAIS

THE POTTERS WIFE *(following left):* While resting for a moment in the backyard of the family's pottery shop, the potter's wife appeared to represent all that is beautiful in Mexico. Photo taken in Oaxaca, Mexico. 📷 PERRI KELLY

PUERTO CABEZAS *(following right):* A young woman cleans up debris after Hurricane Felix. Photo taken in Puerto Cabezas, Nicaragua.
📷 FORWARD EDGE

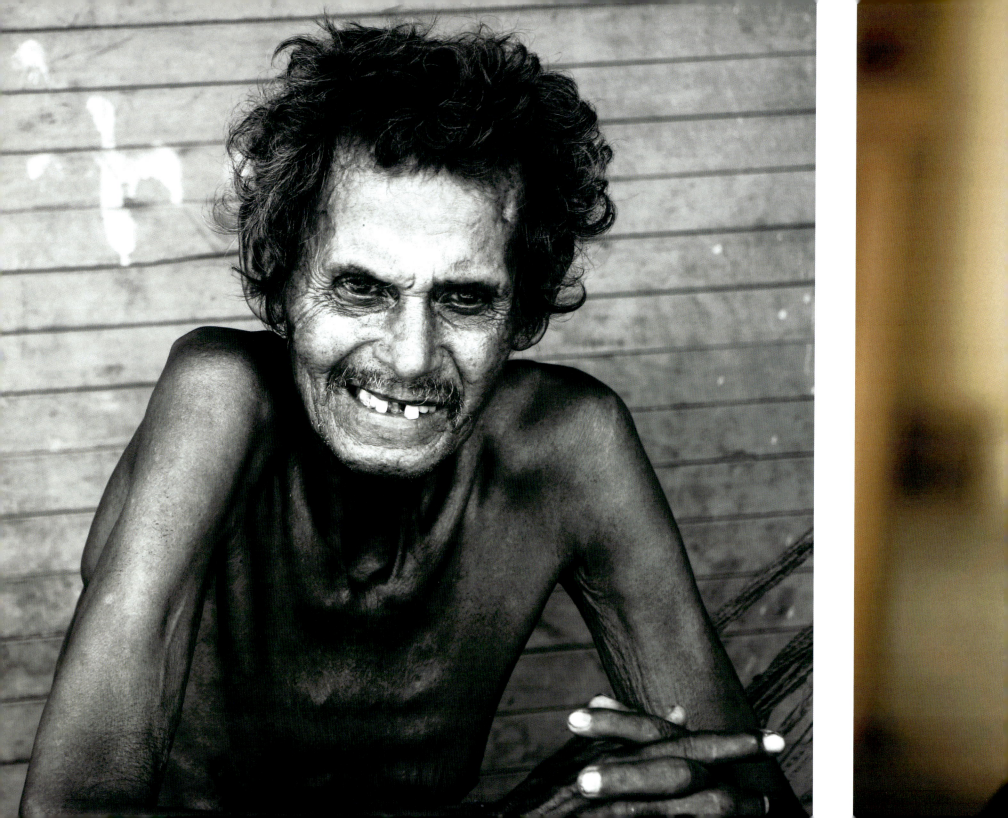

MARIA (above): There is strength and character defined in every line of this woman's face. If we all could portray a life so well lived in our faces, we would be blessed. Photo taken in Mexico. 📷 MARILYN AFFOLTER

MISS PHILLIPS (left): Miss Phillips telling the story of days after the storm. Photo taken in Lower 9th Ward, New Orleans, LA. 📷 KRIS BLAIS

★ **ALMOST DEAD** (previous left): This photo was taken of a man in La Chureca. Photo taken in La Chureca, Managua, Nicaragua. 📷 LUCY MARTIN

★ **MISS LEWIS** (previous right): Miss Lewis laughs as she talks with one of the volunteers during their lunch. Photo taken in Lower 9th Ward, New Orleans, LA. 📷 KRIS BLAIS

STARING INTO THE SUNSET (following left): One of the Masai before he taught us how to make a fire. Photo taken in Amboseli, Kenya. 📷 MARGARET PRATT

MAKE MUSIC IN YOUR HEART. (following right): You had to love this woman. She laughed, smiled and played you a song. Photo taken in San Miquel de Allende, Mexico. 📷 MARILYN AFFOLTER

Prize Winners

When picking from 1,737 photos, it's difficult to nail down what separates the best from the rest—especially when so many are so good. To help, we enlisted a large group of people to vote for their favorite shots. The response was epic: almost 50,000 votes were cast. The voting helped shape what would eventually be published in this book. Along the way, the votes produced the prize winners below. Beyond the obvious and self-explanatory prize categories (Forward Edge International Choice, People's Choice and Most Loves), there are a few we ought to explain:

Consensus Best: This is a combination of the voters' will and our editors' will, so it is a well-balanced and prestigious award. A complicated algorithm determined a photo's score. This award took the photos the algorithm deemed great and pushed them to the top of the pile. Then our editors picked their favorite of that batch. In essence, it's the best of the best.

The Polarizer: Every contest needs a wild card. This is ours. We'd tell you what the parameters were, but we're not real clear on it ourselves. Basically, it's a photo that a lot of people liked, and a lot of people were so-so on... so it's hard to nail down exactly what that means. But hey, it's published and a winner!

The Stable One: This award goes to the photo that stays near the top of the pile for the duration of the contest. It may never be the photo with the most "dig it" votes, or the most loves, or the best score, but it's a photo that has stuck around near the top for a long time.

25th Best: This award goes to the photo that garnered the 25th most "dig it" votes in a chapter. Why 25th place? We've all seen the first-place, blue, fancy-pants ribbon, and the second-place one, and third, and fourth, and so on. But we've never seen a 25th place ribbon. Have you? We think it's time 25th place got some recognition. Plus Forward Edge is celebrating 25 years of ministry, so it seemed fitting.

GRAND PRIZE WINNER
PHOTO BY MARGARET PRATT
page 36

FEI CHOICE IN GETTING THERE
PHOTO BY CHELSEA HINDLEY
page 13

MOST VOTES IN CULTURE
PHOTO BY MARILYN AFFOLTER
page 34

MOST VOTES IN CHILDREN
PHOTO BY JEFF AND KRIS THOMPSON
page 47

FEI CHOICE IN DISASTER RELIEF
PHOTO BY KRIS BLAIS
page 70

MOST VOTES IN VOLUNTEERS
PHOTO BY KRIS BLAIS
page 72

FEI CHOICE IN CONSTRUCTION
PHOTO BY CARL LACASSE
page 108

FEI CHOICE IN HEALTH CARE
PHOTO BY KRIS BLAIS
page 110

MOST VOTES IN PEOPLE
PHOTO BY LUCY MARTIN
page 136

CONSENSUS BEST IN GETTING THERE
PHOTO BY JANICE BARNETT
page 10

MOST LOVES IN CULTURE
PHOTO BY RYAN ANFUSO
page 25

MOST LOVES IN CHILDREN
PHOTO BY ALYSON ROLLINS
page 50

25TH BEST IN DISASTER RELIEF
PHOTO BY KATHLEEN NYBERG
page 71

25TH BEST IN VOLUNTEERS
PHOTO BY RACHEL TITIRIGA
page 78

25TH BEST IN CONSTRUCTION
PHOTO BY PERRI KELLY
page 104

MOST LOVES IN HEALTH CARE
PHOTO BY ALYSON ROLLINS
page 117

CONSENSUS BEST IN PEOPLE
PHOTO BY KRIS BLAIS
page 137

THE POLARIZER IN GETTING THERE
PHOTO BY MARILYN AFFOLTER
page 15

THE POLARIZER IN CULTURE
PHOTO BY MATT HARRIS
page 20

THE STABLE ONE IN CHILDREN
PHOTO BY ALEXANDRA GRACE TAYLOR
page 49

THE POLARIZER IN DISASTER RELIEF
PHOTO BY ASHLEY SHORT
page 71

THE STABLE ONE IN VOLUNTEERS
PHOTO BY AMY UDELL
page 78

THE STABLE ONE IN CONSTRUCTION
PHOTO BY DONNA MOEN
page 106

THE STABLE ONE IN HEALTH CARE
PHOTO BY CRYSTAL CARBONE
page 115

THE STABLE ONE IN PEOPLE
PHOTO BY CARL LACASSE
page 125

Love in Action was made possible by photographers who were willing to share their talents with the rest of us. Here's a list of everyone you'll find in these pages and on the DVD. If you know any of these folks, give them a ring and say thanks for the great book! *(Photographers with Web sites on the right.)*

If you like what you see in the book and on the companion DVD, be sure to check out these photographers' Web sites. A few even sell prints so you may be able to snag your favorite photos from the project to hang on your wall.

Ryan Anfuso
Cindy Aubry
Brodi Ayers
Brent Bailey
Heather Baker
Janice Barnett
M Bartz
Rich Bergstrom
Tony Birnseth
Bob Blankenship
Tj Broom
Beth Burghardt
Mark Burton
Crystal Carbone
Doug Crane
Michael Custer
Gail Dall
Gary Eckelman
Forward Edge
Cindy Evans
Elisha Fieldstadt
Micah Fischer
Kevin Fong
Sonia Frutos
Ronny Gilmore
Natalie Goss
Brandon Gould
Jackie Gray
Ricky Guadarrama
Kimberlie Haggstrom
April Harris
Anna Harvey
Lisa Hekel
Chelsea Hindley
Carolina Karariski
Perri Kelly
Wendy Kelly
Chris Leslie
Lucy Martin

Becca Mashburn
Bob Maurio
Elizabeth Mccarthy
Laurie Mcdowell
Katie Mcgrew
Brooke Mcpherson
Zachary Meerkreebs
Alicia Mehl
Susie Miller
Christie Mongiardo
Paul Morrissey
Dan Osterberg
Brynn Otness
Andrew Page
Lauren Partridge
Haley Peterson
Margaret Pratt
Dustin Ragland
Taryn Ritchey
Carma Roetcisoender
Alyson Rollins
Ashley Short
Meleah Smith
Bob Smith
Tyler Speed
Jaime Speed
Sheri Stanley
Verla Stice
Jeff Taylor
Don Tofte
Michele Tomczak
Tom Udell
Amy Udell
Cemele Vaughn
Jon Watson
Sarah Whaley
Nathaniel Wieck
Kelton Woodburn

Marilyn Affolter
trueimagemarilyn.blogspot.com

Peter Jens Berger
http://peterjensberger.blogspot.com/

Kris Blais
www.urbanedgephotography.net

Hannah Garrett
hannahfromportland.blogspot.com

Matt Harris
www.flickr.com/photos/hestchair/

Steve Hoffmann
http://nicaraguateam2008.blogspot.com/

Kathie Jenkins
proclaiminternational.com

Carl LaCasse
www.flickr.com/photos/carllacasse

Melissa Miller
www.myspace.com/freezethedreams

Donna Moen
donnamoen.com

Don Moen
http://justshortofamazing.com

Kathleen Nyberg
www.katnyberg.com

Carly Ralston
www.lifeisabanquet.wordpress.com

Alexandra Grace Taylor
http://www.alexandragrace7.blogspot.com/

Jeff and Kris Thompson
http://web.mac.com/jeffontheedge/iWeb/Site/Welcome.html

Rachel Titiriga
www.RachelsRomania.BlogSpot.com

Inspired?

Get Involved

Join with us to bring help and hope worldwide to people in desperate need—devastated by disaster, wounded by abuse and exploitation, orphaned by HIV/AIDS, afflicted with disease. It's as simple as putting your Love In Action.

Serve on a Team

Forward Edge International sends teams all over the world, including Kenya, Mexico, and Nicaragua. Domestically we serve hurricane victims in the Gulf Coast and people of the Crow Reservation in Montana.

Sponsor a Child

Children living in La Chureca (a community in the Managua, Nicaragua city dump) are at high risk for malnutrition, abuse and suicide. Many of the girls, some as young as nine-years-old, are forced into prostitution as a means of survival. Join with Forward Edge as we rescue children from the dump and care for them at *Villa Esperanza*, the "Village of Hope". For as a little as a $1 a day you can change a life!

Serve from Home

Party—you can host a "Party for a Purpose" from the comfort of your own home with your own friends. Show them this book, help them experience the need, and help raise awareness and support for the world's most afflicted people.

Pray—pray for those in need in the U.S. and abroad, and for those currently living and working in the field.

Give—consider making regular, monthly or periodic donations that will help Forward Edge continue to send ordinary people into the world to show Christ's Love in Action.

Contact Us

For the most current and detailed information, visit our Web site www.forwardedge.org or contact us at 360.574.3343 or fei@forwardedge.org.